Skunks

Skunks

Wyatt Blassingame

*Illustrated with photographs and
line drawings*

DODD, MEAD & COMPANY
New York

A SKYLIGHT BOOK

For Lee Bancroft Engwall and Caroline Hunter Engwall

Both small and cute, but definitely not skunky

ILLUSTRATION CREDITS

Wyatt Blassingame, 6, 42, 45, 52 (top), 61; Bureau of Sports Fisheries & Wildlife, Department of the Interior, 12 (by Rex Gary Schmidt); Kathi Lee Diamant, 9, 36, 38, 50; Florida Game & Fresh Water Fish Commission, 10 (by William A. Greer), 18 (by Jim Reed), 20 (top), 20 (bottom by Jerry Girvin); Photo by Michigan Department of Natural Resources, 28, 54; Photo by Carolyn Norwood, The Islander, 40; Outdoor Photographers League Photo by Lynwood M. Chace, 23; Outdoor Photographers League Photo by Ed Park, 34; Outdoor Photographers League Photo by Robert Riddell, Jr., 48; Outdoor Photographers League Photo by Don Shiner, 52 (bottom); Leonard Lee Rue III, 8, 15, 27, 32, 53, 55, 57; U.S. Fish & Wildlife Service, 60 (by Luther C. Goldman); Irene Vandermolen, c/o Leonard Rue Enterprises, 59.

1 2 3 4 5 6 7 8 9 10

Library of Congress Cataloging in Publication Data

Blassingame, Wyatt.
  Skunks.

  (A Skylight book)
  Includes index.
  SUMMARY: Discusses general characteristics of
skunks, various species, skunks as pets, and the
mustelid family to which this little animal with
the powerful weapon belongs.
  1. Skunks—Juvenile literature. [1. Skunks]
             I. Title.
  QL737.C25B58   599.74′47   80-21555
             ISBN 0-396-07909-1

Contents

1

The Skunk

A wild, fully grown skunk will weigh about eight pounds. It moves slowly, with a kind of waddle. It has no poisonous fangs like those of a snake. Its teeth are small; its claws are strong but not particularly sharp. It would seem to be one of the most defenseless animals in the world.

Yet if this kitten-sized skunk was ambling along a forest trail and came face to face with a six-foot-tall, 350-pound black bear, the bear, probably, would step respectfully aside and let the skunk have the right of way.

However, if this particular bear happened to be young and inexperienced, it might stop in its tracks and stare down at the skunk.

This skunk is digging in the grass and old leaves for insects that in the wild make up a large majority of its food.

When danger approaches the skunk will stamp its front feet, hump its back, and hiss. This is a warning that it had best be left alone. Only when convinced it has no other escape does the skunk use its ultimate weapon.

The striped skunk getting into position to fire its highly effective, though not deadly, defensive weapon.

The skunk, in turn, would stop and look up at the bear. Now this bear, being young and ignorant, might decide the skunk was worth eating and start forward. If so, the skunk would stamp its tiny front feet. As the bear came closer, the skunk would stamp again and make a hissing noise, warning the bear to keep away. The skunk would then lift its beautiful, bushy, black-and-white tail high over its back. It would twist its small body into a U-shape, so that both its face and rear end were pointed toward the bear.

The black bear is many times larger than the skunk, but if they meet in the forest, the bear usually steps out of the skunk's way.

And if the bear kept coming the skunk would fire from its rear end—straight at the bear's face—a strange but highly effective weapon: a yellowish, oily liquid that broke quickly into a mist. Tiny drops would strike the bear's eyes, its mouth, its nose.

And the bear, temporarily blinded, making roaring noises of

mingled surprise and pain, would depart as fast as possible. The skunk would continue its slow, dignified stroll, just as though nothing at all had happened. And if the two ever met again, the bear would step politely out of the way.

It is this strange, "skunky" weapon—a smell so powerful it can be actually sickening—for which the skunk is most famous. But the little animal has many other interesting qualities. Indeed, the skunk is well worth knowing about. And the more we know about it, the more interesting it becomes.

THE SKUNK SPECIES

All skunks are scientifically classed as mammals. That is, they have backbones and the females bring forth living young that are then nursed by the mother. More specifically, skunks are divided into ten or more species. But the difference between some of these is so minor that only an expert can tell one from the other. However, there are three groups, or genera, of skunks that may be easily identified. These are the striped skunk, the spotted skunk, and the hog-nosed skunk. Of these, the striped skunk is by far the most common in the United States. Most of what can be written about it also will apply to the others. So let's take the striped skunk first.

2

The Striped Skunk

The scientific name of the striped skunk is *Mephitis mephitis*.
Mephitis means "foul" or "evil smelling," and *Mephitis mephitis*
means "double the stink." Algonquin Indians called the skunk
Segonku. Just what that meant is uncertain, but from it early
English settlers got the name "skunk." French-Canadian trappers
gave it another name, *Enfant du diable*, the "child of the devil."
Today in many parts of the United States skunks are called polecats. Scientifically, however, polecats (*Mustela putorius*) are European relatives of the American skunk and the direct ancestors of
the domesticated ferret. In some parts of the country skunks are
also known as "woodpussies."

A striped skunk

Whatever it is called, the striped skunk is a handsome little animal. About twelve to sixteen inches from nose to rump, it has a plumelike tail almost as long as its body. The fur is sleek and glossy. The nose is white; the rest of the face is black, except for a white stripe that runs from the nose across the top of the head to the shoulders. Here the stripe splits in two parts, one running down each side of the body. All the rest of the body is black. The tail is usually carried curled over the back, like a black-and-white banner.

Now and then this pattern may vary. Occasionally the white stripes may be much broader than average, or they may be more narrow. I once found the body of a pure black skunk at the foot of a palm tree. Looking up I saw a great horned owl staring down at me from its nest.

Striped skunks live from as far north as Hudson Bay in Canada all the way to northern Mexico. They may be found in all forty-eight of the touching United States. They make their homes not only in rural areas, but sometimes in towns and even in cities. Indeed, skunks have been found living happily in the middle of New York City. Wherever they live, they are approached with great care by anyone who knows about them.

This striped skunk is getting ready to fire at an enemy.

How the Skunk "Skunks"

The skunk has two glands embedded in muscle, one on each side of the anus. Normally these glands are carried inside the animal's body, but when the skunk is angry or in danger the glands protrude, much like the nozzles of tiny water hoses. If the danger keeps getting closer, the skunk bends its body into a U-shape, both ends facing the danger. The tail is raised straight up, out of the way. Finally, the skunk contracts the muscles around the glands. This fires jets of oily, yellowish fluid. Because the glands protrude slightly before firing, none of this fluid gets on the skunk. Apparently the skunk itself doesn't like the smell any more than other animals do.

Naturalists disagree on just how far a skunk can shoot its fluid, since nobody has wanted to measure this very carefully. Probably this first jet can carry about five to eight feet. There is also disagreement about just how accurate a marksman the skunk can be. Some persons swear that a skunk can make a direct hit on the eyes and nose of a troublesome dog, or person, ten feet away. But certainly the fluid breaks quickly into a fine mist that covers a larger and larger area as it drifts downwind. Close to the skunk, it will stick and cling to whatever it touches, a sickening odor that will last for days and even weeks. Close contact will not only cause a painful burning of the eyes and nose, it can cause temporary blindness. Drifting downwind, it can be smelled for a half mile or more.

John James Audubon, the famous naturalist and artist, liked to tell a story about a country preacher who suffered badly from asthma. Quite by accident he discovered that one whiff of skunk musk would clear his lungs for hours. After this he carried with him a small, tightly corked vial containing several drops of the musk. Once while giving a sermon the preacher felt an attack of asthma coming on. He took the vial from his pocket, uncorked it, and waved it back and forth under his nose. This not only cleared his lungs, it cleared the church. When he was ready to continue the sermon, the entire congregation had departed, in a hurry.

Audubon's story may not be exactly true, but it is true that a chemically made version of skunk musk is sometimes placed in pipelines carrying natural gas in order to discover a leak. Natural gas is invisible and has no odor. A leak of this gas would be hard to find. But wherever the skunk musk leaks into the air, everybody in the neighborhood knows about it.

If need be, the skunk can fire its musk five, or even six, times in a row. The first discharge, however, is always the strongest, and after the fifth or sixth the animal must wait until its glands create more fluid. On the other hand, the skunk is a peace-loving animal. It never uses its awesome weapon except in self-defense.

There is no really good way to remove the skunk's odor from an animal or from clothing that has been well sprayed. There is an old folk story that the best way to remove the skunk smell from clothing is to bury the clothes for a week, dig them up, wash in

vinegar—and then throw them away. Actually washing in vinegar will help somewhat. So will washing in stale beer, or tomato juice.

I have a friend with a large white dog that simply cannot learn to leave skunks alone. Everyone in the neighborhood knows when dog and skunk have made contact, not only because of the dog's odor but also because its owner then bathes it in tomato juice. For weeks afterwards the dog, a bright pink color, slinks about looking ashamed of itself.

Strange as it may seem, very tiny amounts of musk are used in making the most expensive perfumes. The musk helps the perfume hold its odor for a long time.

The Skunk's Enemies

The skunk's distinctive black-and-white markings make it easy to recognize. Most animals—despite my friend's stupid dog—soon learn to leave it strictly alone. Now and then a very hungry bobcat or fox may attack a skunk, but this is rare. In the wild the one real enemy of the skunk is the great horned owl. Strangely, this owl

Except for automobiles, the great horned owl is the most deadly enemy of the skunk.

Next to the great horned owl, the bobcat and the fox are probably the greatest natural enemies of the skunk.

seems immune to the skunk's odor. Or maybe it just doesn't care.

Both the skunk and the owl hunt chiefly at night. The skunk moves slowly, without fear of most animals big enough to kill and eat it. And the great horned owl, plunging silently from the sky on wings that may measure five feet from tip to tip, can drive its claws through the skunk's body with a single strike.

Even so, the owl's swiftness does not always keep it from being sprayed. The owl then may carry the skunk's odor for weeks. If you are in the woods or open fields at night and get a sudden smell of skunk—a smell that disappears as quickly as it came—the chances are it was not a skunk but a great horned owl that had fed on skunk.

But it is man and the man-made automobile that are by far the skunk's most deadly enemies. Frequently skunks prowl the highways at night, feeding on insects, frogs, and other creatures killed by passing cars. When a skunk sees the headlights of an approaching auto, it expects the car to give him the right of way just as another animal would do. Unless the driver sees the skunk and stops to let it amble on in peace, the result can be disaster, for both skunk and auto.

There is the story of a driver who, having encountered a skunk, went immediately to a car wash. Later his bill read: "Car wash $3.50. Letting car in our building $10.00."

Because of its handsome black-and-white fur, skunks were once highly valued by trappers. Called Alaskan sable or black marten, the furs sold for high prices. Since the wild skunk is more curious than intelligent, it was easily trapped. As a result the skunk population soon faced extinction.

But the skunk's fame for being skunky saved it. The government passed a law that furs used for clothing had to be honestly labeled. And where women liked to wear coats of Alaskan sable, a coat of skunk fur somehow didn't seem as handsome. The price of skunk fur went down and many trappers lost interest.

FAMILY LIFE

Most of its life the skunk is a rather solitary, independent, self-sufficient animal. This is particularly true of the males. Females, at least part of the time, lead a somewhat more social life, especially in winter.

Skunks do not hibernate in the winter, as do such animals as woodchucks and flying squirrels. In fact, winter makes very little

This raccoon, about to crawl into a hollow log to hibernate, is a little disturbed to find a skunk as a close companion. In cold climates, both the raccoon and the skunk will den up for the winter—but not together.

difference in the life of a southern skunk. But in the north, where snow often covers the ground, skunks, like raccoons, retire into dark, cozy dens. These may be in hollow trees, but more likely they are underground burrows beneath piles of rock or fallen trees.

Since the skunk wants its burrows to stay not only warm, but dry, they are often dug under houses or barns. Here the skunk causes no trouble, so long as it is left alone. Forest rangers have often had skunks take up quarters beneath their houses. Here they sleep away the coldest days and nights. If the weather turns warm, they waddle out to search for food, then go back to sleep again.

Male skunks usually have dens of their own, spending the winter alone. So do most females. Sometimes, however, several females may spend the winter together. This is usually in twos or threes. But if the den is particularly large and comfortable, and the area rich in food supply, a dozen or more females have been known to set up a kind of apartment house for the winter. Even so, since most of the time is spent sound asleep, it isn't a very social life.

With the first spring thaws, the male skunks leave their dens to go hunting. But now they are hunting more for a mate than for food. At this time the male may wander for several miles in one night, a long way indeed for such a slow, short-legged animal. And this is the one time in a skunk's life that it is not an altogether peace-loving animal. Where two males are courting the same female there is likely to be fighting. Sometimes this is so fierce it may leave one of the males crippled or even dead. Also this is the one time that the skunk itself may smell skunky—in desperation one skunk may spray the other, and be sprayed in return. As mentioned, the skunk doesn't like skunk smell any more than other animals do.

THE YOUNG

After mating, the male wanders away. If he should meet the female and his own young later in the summer he, apparently, does not recognize them.

If the weather is cold, the female remains in her den until later in the spring. Some two months after mating, usually about May or early June, she will give birth to a litter of tiny, blind, hairless kittens. As a rule these number four to six, but there is a record of one skunk having sixteen kittens in one litter. However, the female can nurse only six at one time. In large litters some of the weaker kittens usually starve.

When the baby skunks are three weeks old they open their eyes for the first time. By now they are growing the soft, black-and-white fur they will wear all their lives. And, probably, it is about this same time they first begin to develop the musk glands that will be their protection throughout life.

By the time the young are one month old they can walk, or at least totter, about the den. Another two weeks or so and they are strong enough to follow their mother when she goes hunting for food.

Since skunks hunt chiefly at night, it is usually after dark when the young first leave their den. They do not go galloping off in different directions as a litter of puppies might do. Instead, the mother leads the way and the young follow in single file. This is a strange sight indeed—small, black-and-white balls of fur moving in a slow, wavering line through the early evening darkness.

This single file formation is probably for the babies' protection. Small, slow, and not yet sure of how to defend themselves, the young would be easy prey for most predators. But under the watchful eye of the mother they are safe from almost any danger, except the great horned owl and the automobile.

All through the early summer female skunks are very maternal. Both wild and captive females have been known to adopt orphan young, raising them as their own. Night after night she leads them out of the den, teaching them how to defend themselves if necessary, and how to hunt for food.

As a rule, each female has her own territory. Each night, with ∩f small fry close behind, she follows more or less the same

A striped skunk digging for insects.

route. Her diet is as varied as that of the raccoon. That is, she will
eat almost anything edible.

In the early summer, insects are plentiful and the skunk dines
chiefly on these. She goes scratching under bushes and through tall
grass looking for crickets, roaches, grasshoppers, insects of all
kinds. If she finds a bee she eats it happily, and if she gets stung it
doesn't seem to trouble her. She eats mice if she can catch them,
which isn't too often. Also frogs. The striped skunk cannot climb
to hunt for bird nests, but if it finds a quail or whippoorwill nest

This well-fed striped skunk is probably looking for a place to den up for the winter. Its den is likely to be under someone's house or a burrow beneath a pile of rocks.

on the ground, it will eat both eggs and young. Even so, insects make up well over half its diet. Ernest Thompson Seton, the famous naturalist—he also helped start the Boy Scouts of America—once wrote that every skunk was the "guardian angel" of a half acre of garden because of the insects it destroyed.

By late summer the young born that spring have learned how to hunt for themselves. One by one they begin to wander off, each searching for a territory of its own. By autumn the mother is, usually, once more alone.

With fall the skunk's appetite grows sharper. This is true of both young and adult skunks. They are instinctively building up body fat on which to live during the cold, snowbound months ahead. To their summer diet they add berries, grain, and any nuts they can crack. They hunt the roads for snakes, turtles, almost anything else killed by passing cars. Growing steadily hungrier, they may take to visiting garbage dumps.

Skunks have been accused of raiding hen houses, killing adult chickens as well as the young, and stealing eggs. And it is true that skunks have been known to kill chickens. But actually this is quite rare. When scientists of the U. S. Department of Agriculture examined the stomachs of 1,700 skunks they found that more than half the food consisted of insects. The rest was fruit, grain, and small animals. In these skunks they found no chicken remains at all.

Some of the skunk's relatives, such as martens and mink, do frequently raid hen houses for food. It may be that the skunk is sometimes blamed for the actions of its more violent relatives.

By early winter the skunk is, or ought to be, well padded with fat. As the weather grows still colder it spends more and more time in its den, sleeping away the nights as well as the days.

THE HOODED SKUNK

The hooded skunk (*Mephitis macroura*) is found throughout most of Central America and north into Arizona. Actually there is very little difference between it and *Mephitis mephitis*, its striped relative. The hooded skunk does have a sprinkling of black hairs throughout its white stripes, and its tail is usually the same length as its body. In the striped skunk the tail may be just a little bit shorter than the body. Also there are times when the whole back of the hooded skunk turns as white as its stripes.

3

The Spotted Skunk

The spotted skunk looks very much like its striped cousin. One look and you'll know it's a skunk. There are, however, some important differences between *Spilogale putorius,* the spotted skunk, and its striped cousin.

The spotted skunk is smaller, rarely weighing over four pounds. They live just about everywhere that striped skunks do. Yet almost everybody has seen a striped skunk at one time or another, but very few persons have seen the spotted skunk. In fact, many people don't even know there is such an animal. There are several reasons. The spotted skunk almost never comes out of hiding until it is dark. Even then it is much more secretive than its striped cousin. Also it is smaller and faster. Anyone who caught only a

nighttime glimpse of a spotted skunk vanishing into bushes might easily mistake it for the striped skunk.

Even people who have seen spotted skunks often don't know its real name. In many parts of the country the spotted skunk is called a civet cat. Or sometimes it is called a polecat, a name often used for the striped skunk as well.

Like *Mephitis mephitis*, the spotted skunk is all black and white. But on the spotted skunk the white stripes move in wavering broken lines. Some lines run along the skunk's body, some go up and down. And always there is a white dot in the middle of the forehead.

Spotted skunks are about the size of kittens, and they are like kittens in many ways. Young spotted skunks will play together like a family of kittens. Even the adults play. Two may face one another standing on their hind legs—or even on their front legs—and appear to be boxing. Not in anger, but just in play. Also they can and do climb trees, which the larger, slower, striped skunk cannot do.

The spotted skunk has stripes moving in wavering lines and a dot in the middle of its forehead.

33

This baby spotted skunk is small enough to be held in cupped hands.

Spotted skunks will eat just about anything striped skunks will eat. Strangely, they seem to be particularly fond of snakes. Bits of snakeskin are often found near the dens of spotted skunks. Whether the spotted skunk is partially immune to the venom of rattlesnakes, or whether it is just too fast for the snake, is uncertain. But it is certain that spotted skunks have been known to kill rattlesnakes. Several years ago a movie was made of this and shown to rangers of the U. S. Fish and Wildlife Service.

The striped skunk, as mentioned, rarely raids chicken houses, and when it does, it appears to kill only for food. The spotted skunk, however, is more like its relatives, the minks and weasels. One spotted skunk has been known to kill twenty-eight fully grown chickens in a single night.

Because of its small size, the spotted skunk will often find a hen egg too large to crack with its teeth. If so, the skunk may kick the egg around until it hits a rock and breaks.

The spotted skunk has a musk gland on each side of its anus just as does the striped skunk. And its musk smells just as horrible as does that of double-stink *Mephitis mephitis*. But the spotted skunk delivers its perfume in a strangely different way.

If threatened by danger the spotted skunk also will stamp its

The spotted skunk doing its hand-stand before firing.

front feet and hiss. If the danger comes closer it will raise its tail as a final warning.

Next comes the difference.

The tiny spotted skunk turns its back on its danger. It stands upright on its front feet, tail hoisted well out of the way. It turns its head to one side in order to see to take aim. And from this position it lets fly.

36

4

The Hog-nosed Skunk

Not a great deal is known about the hog-nosed skunk. And that's too bad, because what is known sounds interesting.

There are six species, all belonging to the genus, or group, scientists call *Conepatus*. A few are found in the southwestern United States, but chiefly they live in Central and South America. In fact, they are the only skunks found in South America. In most ways they are very much like their striped relatives of North America.

The chief difference between the six species of hog-nosed skunks seem to be in size. Some are as small as the striped skunk of the United States, but others are almost twice as big. All have broad, hairless muzzles, somewhat like that of a hog. With these, they go rooting along the ground looking for insects.

The hog-nosed skunk

At least one species of hog-nosed skunk, *Conepatus chilensis*, appears to be completely immune to the venom of many snakes, including rattlers. Konrad Guenther, a German naturalist exploring the jungles of Brazil, wrote that, "This animal . . . hunts the venomous snakes of the country, eating them, with the greatest complacency, from the tail upwards, while the reptile, with open jaws, desperately strikes at its enemy. The Cangamba, as the Brazilians call the skunk, is quite unperturbed."

American naturalists have learned that rattlesnakes retreat from the odor of the hog-nosed skunk as hurriedly as would a human being. It is quite possible the rattlers have learned that the odor is not only unpleasant—it can mean a deadly danger for the snake.

This skunk, unlike many, proved to be an affectionate pet with no bad habit of nipping its owner. Pet skunks have been known to live ten years and even longer, but it is doubtful a wild skunk would live that long.

5

The Skunk as a Pet

If you want a pet that is both a friend and companion, a pet that you can feel affection for and be sure that it in turn feels affection for you, get a dog. Do not get a skunk.

But if you want a pet that will make people stop and stare, a pet you can't be sure of from one minute to the next, but one that is always interesting, then—maybe—the skunk is the pet for you.

By nature the skunk is a wild animal. Even when born and raised in captivity it remains, basically, a wild creature. It may adapt to life with human beings; it will learn very quickly where its food comes from. But in its heart it stays wild, independent. And it is this very quality that makes the skunk such an interesting pet for some people.

Practically all pet skunks are bought from pet stores. These in

Actually this pet skunk has been "deskunked" and can eject no fluid. But if annoyed, it still pretends. Here it is giving its last warning with tail raised and both its rear end and one eye toward the approaching photographer.

turn get them from "skunk ranches" where the animals are bred in captivity. Some states require a permit for owning a skunk, so check with the store owner about this when you buy your pet.

When the baby skunk is about two months old a veterinarian may clip the little nozzles from which the musk is shot, or he may remove the musk glands entirely. Either way, from this time on, the skunk is unable to fire its musk. Even so, if frightened or angry it will still stamp its feet, make hissing noises, and raise its tail as if about to fire.

A very young skunk brought into a new home should be given a den somewhat like the one it might have had in the wild. This could be a box about 12″ x 12″ x 18″, with an entrance about six inches in diameter. It should have a hinged top so you can reach in when necessary, and there should be a bedding of soft cloth or shredded newspapers. The den can be put inside a larger cage, if the pet is to be kept from roaming the house.

That may be a problem. A baby skunk is smaller than it looks inside its handsome black-and-white fur coat. It can squeeze in and out of amazingly small spaces. And out of its cage, in a new home, it will almost certainly hide. This may be under the refrigerator, under the sofa, far back in a corner behind old boxes or anything else it can get behind. Here it is likely to stay, refusing to come out, until it is hungry.

Wild skunks, as mentioned, feed chiefly at night. The young skunk in captivity will do the same. It may stay in its hiding place all day, despite being called. Food placed in the open may go untouched until darkness. Of course as the skunk gets older, as it gets used to its new home, it will feel safer. It will come out more in the daytime. But even when fully grown it will remain most active at night. Just about the time you are ready for bed is when your pet wants to play. During the day it may curl up in your lap and sleep. It may even play hide-and-seek like a puppy. For awhile. Then it will go back to its den. This may be a corner in a closet, or under a desk, or inside an overturned wastebasket. But one thing is almost certain: it will be in a spot the skunk has chosen, not one you picked out for it. Skunks are stubborn animals.

HOUSEBREAKING AND HEALTH CARE

The pet skunk may be as stubborn about its bathroom habits as about choosing a den. On the whole skunks are very clean animals. Nearly always they will keep their dens clean. And since the skunk is no larger than a housecat, the only bathroom it will need is a folded newspaper or litter box. The only trouble will be in getting your pet to use what you have given it—*in the spot you have selected*.

Brought into a new home the baby skunk will soon choose a certain corner for its bathroom. And it will go to this corner

Although kept as a pet, this skunk has a bad habit of nipping almost anyone who picks it up.

regularly. If you put the newspaper or litter box here, the skunk will use it. When the pet is accustomed to this, you can move the box to a place you have chosen—and the skunk may, or may not, follow. The stubborn creature may keep right on going to the spot it originally chose.

If so, it may be necessary to build a wall with boxes, or a high pile of books, something that will keep the skunk from reaching the place it has chosen. Usually then it will go to the place you have put its litter box.

As a rule skunks are not only clean, but healthy. Being clean they are less likely to have internal parasites, such as hookworms and tapeworms, than are dogs and cats. But the skunk can have both and so should be checked now and then by a veterinarian. Also the skunk can have both dog and cat distemper and should be inoculated against both.

It is very important that the pet skunk be inoculated against rabies. In the wild, skunks are among the animals most likely to have rabies. Many skunks go into caves to feed on baby bats that have fallen on the cave floor. Bats often carry rabies and the skunks, bitten while hunting for the young, get the disease. Also, skunks expect every other animal, from a bear to a mouse, to get out of its way. So if a skunk meets a rabid dog or fox, the skunk does not try to escape. And the rabid animal doesn't care what the skunk smells like. So skunks, more than most wild animals, are in danger of getting rabies.

There is still another danger. Some veterinarians now believe that the skunk, unlike any other animal in the world, may carry the rabies germ without itself being killed by the disease. If so, the skunk might appear to be healthy and at the same time its bite could cause rabies.

Feeding the Pet

If you buy a young skunk from a pet store, the store's owner can tell you what the skunk has been fed. Most likely it is a dry cat food. The young skunk can thrive on this. Just make sure that the cat food you buy is a complete, balanced diet. If it is, this will be on the label.

However, if you should buy a very young skunk before it can eat normally, then it should be fed in the same way you would feed a very young raccoon, or fox or a puppy. For this, mix the yolk of one or two eggs with a half pint of milk. If you add a teaspoon of honey the baby is likely to take to it more quickly. But once a baby skunk has learned to like the sweet formula, it may refuse to take the food unsweetened. The formula may be fed using a baby bottle and nipple. If the baby animal won't, or can't, suck on the nipple, use an eyedropper. Open the pet's mouth and put the formula in, a drop or two at a time.

By the time the baby skunk can walk, it should be ready to change its eating habits. To help with this, mix a little of the formula with canned dog food for a week or two. After that you can move on to the cat food, which the young skunk may prefer.

While wild animals can never become pets like dogs or cats, skunks can sometimes be more than friendly. Here Hal Gras of Tucson, Arizona, is shown feeding a tidbit to a hungry skunk.

Once past babyhood, the pet skunk should be no trouble to feed. Indeed, it will eat almost anything: meat scraps, fruit, insects, potatoes, milk, ice cream, along with its cat or dog food. However, there may be one or two problems.

If your pet finds one food that it particularly likes—this might be ice cream, or bacon, or just about anything—and if you keep giving this to your pet, it may decide to eat nothing else. Then you must withhold its favorite food until it gets hungry enough to eat other things.

It is far more likely, however, that the pet skunk will, given the chance, eat far too much of everything it can. An adult wild skunk will weigh about eight pounds. The pet may keep eating until it weighs ten, or twelve, or even fourteen pounds.

It is natural for the wild skunk to stuff itself in the autumn, preparing for snowbound months ahead. In captivity the skunk feels the same impulse. But in a warm house it does not work hard finding its food, nor does it sleep for days and weeks on end without food. Instead, it keeps eating, getting fatter. At best the short-legged skunk tends to waddle when it walks. In captivity it may get too fat even to waddle.

The owner who cares about his pet will have to watch its diet.

OTTER

MINK

STRIPED SKUNK

LONGTAILED WEASEL

WOLVERINE

AMERICAN BADGER

KLD

Part of the family circle of the skunk.

9

The Skunk's Relatives

Left alone, the skunk is one of the most peaceful of all animals—except, maybe, where snakes are concerned. The same thing, unfortunately, cannot be said for many of its close relatives.

Scientifically, skunks belong to the family Mustelidae—called the mustelids. This family includes such animals as mink, otter, marten, fisher, weasel, badger, and wolverine. All of them have musk glands on each side of the anus, just as do skunks. All can give off a nasty odor. But none of the others has the truly championship smell of the skunk. Nor do they use this as a weapon as the skunk does.

The mustelids vary considerably in size as well as looks. An adult wolverine may be over three feet long and weigh forty

Otters are always playful.

Despite its small size, the weasel can be ferocious, as shown here displaying its dislike of the photographer.

The American badger has powerful legs and very long, strong claws with which it digs deep, complicated burrows. Fully grown it will be about three feet long, including a six-inch tail. It will eat grass and roots, but prefers meat.

pounds. But the female least weasel may be fully grown at no more than six inches long and weighing one ounce. This least weasel is the smallest of all predatory mammals. Ounce for ounce it is also one of the fiercest. Indeed, its only competition in this way may come from some of its mustelid relatives.

Many poultry farmers hate the mink, the weasel, marten, and

Left: About two feet long, including the tail, the mink is larger than the weasel, and can be equally fierce. It is most famous, however, for its beautiful fur, a rich chestnut brown, except for a white patch on the chin.

Right: The long-tailed weasels are the biggest of the three species found in North America. Even so, a fully grown male will weigh less than one pound.

The American marten is one of the few mustelids that takes easily to the treetops. Very fast, it catches and eats squirrels. On the ground it hunts for mice and shrews.

other mustelids because of the terrible destruction they sometimes cause. They have been known to sneak into poultry houses and kill literally hundreds of chickens, young ducks, or turkeys. They appear to do this out of the sheer joy of killing since the animal will go away leaving the torn, mutilated bodies uneaten. In fact, the mustelid may in a single night kill more than it could actually eat in six months.

Even so, there is an at least partial explanation.

Weasels, mink, fishers, most of the mustelids, have long, slender bodies. Because of this they lose body heat more rapidly than would an animal with a shorter, more compact body. And every animal, including man, manufactures its heat from the food it eats. So these mustelids need more food than would some other animals of the same weight. Also, these mustelids are chiefly flesh-eaters that must capture and kill their food. This in turn requires more energy, and still more food.

Since these mustelids have such an intense need of food, it is instinctive to kill as much at one time as possible. In the vast majority of cases this would not be very much more than the predator could eat. Then the mink or weasel eats what it can and hides the rest, where it can return and feed later. Of course in the case of hen-house slaughter, the killer could never drag away and hide all

This wolverine was caught raiding a wilderness cabin by the returning trapper. Notice the powerful teeth and claws. The largest and most dangerous of North American mustelids it has been known to kill deer after dropping on them from tree limbs.

it has killed. Here the sheer instinct to kill food when it is available seems to take over.

The wolverine may not be, ounce for ounce, as deadly as the weasel, but it is heartily disliked by many trappers and farmers. Like its smaller mustelid cousins, it sometimes raids barnyards, killing far more than it can eat. In fact, thirty- and forty-pound wolverines have been known to kill deer. One may drop out of a tree onto a deer's neck, then bite and claw until the deer falls from lack of blood. Wolverines have been known to raid the cabins of trappers, overturning tables, chairs, tearing open boxes, and messing things up generally.

Such raids are probably done for food, but the wolverine has one trick nobody can explain. Raiding a cabin, they have been known to carry away pots, pans, canned food, even guns. These they drag off into the woods and bury.

Why? Nobody knows, but many woodsmen swear it is done out of pure meanness.

Despite its name, the skunk is still sometimes trapped for the beauty of its black-and-white fur. But even at its best this fur has never been able to compete with that of some other mustelids such as the mink, sable, and short-tailed weasel. A woman's coat made of these furs would cost many thousands of dollars. The fur of the short-tailed weasel, like that of the skunk, might lose some of its value if it went by its common name. But the scientific name of the short-tailed weasel is *Mustela erminea,* and so its fur is called ermine. The fur is a rich brown in summer. In winter it is pure white, except for a black tip on its tail.

The short-tailed weasel is small—weighing less than half a pound—fierce, and beautiful. A rich chestnut brown in the summer, its coat is pure white in winter, except for the black tip on its tail.

One of the rare species, this alert black-footed ferret is shown looking over the prairie dog town where it lives in Mellett County, South Dakota.

One of the strangest of the skunk's relatives is the little ferret. Or maybe it would be better to say, "Two of the skunk's strange relatives are ferrets." Because there are two ferrets. One of these, the black-footed ferret (*Mustela nigripes*) was once plentiful. About two feet long, it had a red head, a black mask almost like that of a raccoon, and a dark stripe down its back. It lived near the once huge prairie dog towns of the Great Plains of the United States and fed almost entirely on the prairie dogs. But as settlers and cities caused the prairie dogs to disappear, the black-footed ferrets disappeared also. Today the black-footed ferret is very rare indeed.

The other ferret, and the more common one today, is a direct descendent of the European polecat (*Mustela putorius*). The European polecat had an odor much like that of the American skunk. But it was very good at keeping rats and mice out of houses. It was also great at hunting rabbits. So over the centuries men developed a domesticated polecat with less odor and called it the ferret. This ferret would not only kill mice, it would dig into a rabbit's burrow or follow it into a hollow tree. And instead of eating the rabbit, the pet ferret drove it into the open where it could be shot or netted by a human hunter.

Even so, ferrets as pets present an even greater problem than skunks. They have teeth like needles, and many never get over the impulse to bite when handled.

This ferret is a domesticated relative of the skunk. But not all make good pets. They tend to bite when handled.

The names of at least three mustelids have become part of the English language with different meanings. The word "ferret" means to hunt hard for something. To "ferret out the facts" is to keep working, trying to learn the truth. It would be a compliment to a detective or lawyer or scientist to say he was a real ferret at his work. But if you said the same man was a real weasel, he might hit you.

Now the weasel will also chase rabbits and other small game through burrows and rock piles and hollow trees just as well as a ferret. But the word "weasel" means to be sneaky. To "weasel out of a situation" is to get out by some tricky, cowardly method.

Could this be because the animal ferret works for the human hunter, but the weasel works for itself?

And there is the word "skunk." It now has two meanings besides being the name of *Mephitis mephitis*. One meaning is easy to understand. A really disagreeable person, a real "stinker," is called a skunk. But "to skunk" also means to win a game without allowing your opponent to score. If you win a tennis set six-love, or a baseball game five to nothing, you have "skunked" your opponent.

How did it get that meaning?

I don't know. What do you think?

Index